RAMSGATE
AND
THANET LIFE
IN OLD PHOTOGRAPHS

RAMSGATE SANDS STATION in the early 1900s. There was a turntable just behind he wall in the foreground of this photograph.

RAMSGATE
AND
THANET LIFE
IN OLD PHOTOGRAPHS

_____ COMPILED BY _____
D.R.J. PERKINS

ALAN SUTTON
1989

Alan Sutton Publishing
Gloucester

First published 1989

British Library Cataloguing in Publication Data

Ramsgate and Thanet life in old photographs.
1. Kent. Thanet (District), history
I. Perkins, D.J.
942.2'357

ISBN 0-86299-545-0

Typesetting and origination by
Alan Sutton Publishing
Printed in Great Britain by
Dotesios Printers Limited

CONTENTS

INTRODUCTION

The history of Ramsgate and the Thanet towns we know today roughly coincides with the history of photography. When Louis Daguerre made the first practical photographs in 1837 our resort towns were in the process of being built. Around 15 years later, some nameless practitioner of the new collodian process made a series of prints of Ramsgate Harbour as a commercial venture, subsequently publishing them as an album of views. They were among the first topographical photographs taken anywhere. From that moment on, shutters have never ceased to click. Cameras became smaller, cheaper, easier to use. As they did so, generations of Thanet folk and visitors registered personal identity and moments of pleasure and pride.

Here are assembled some 250 old photographs. Of people, their daily vistas, trades, transport, and of random moments in their lives. Due to a wealth of available material, Broadstairs and St Peter's will be dealt with in a separate volume to appear shortly. The compiler of this collection is a Ramsgate man, of local stock. If, therefore, any innate prejudices should be detected by the reader, either in choice of subject, comments or captions, then so be it!

Firstly, to set the scene; people have lived in the Isle of Thanet for perhaps five thousand years. For about 96 per cent of that time, local folk were 'fishermen with ploughs'. Their homes were tiny farmsteads and hamlets with a few larger settlements where stream-cut valleys met the line of chalk cliffs. Not until the eighteenth century did three such settlements outgrow their parent villages of St Lawrence, St John's and St Peter's and assume town status.

Restoration Thanet consisted of three 'towns' and four villages. To give some idea of scale, the map of Ramsgate in John Lewis' *History of Thanet* (1730), shows a settlement about the size of modern St Nicholas, suggesting a population of perhaps 500 persons. With farming and fishing as the chief occupations, the Ramsgate and Margate men also engaged in shipbuilding, pilotage and 'hovelling' (assisting ships in trouble, salvaging wrecks, etc.). Margate became known for brewing, Ramsgate for its trade with Russia and both for their salt cod, secured from the farthest parts of the North Sea by local luggers. The most pernickety of historians would have to agree, however, that the latter occupations were probably minor compared with an enthusiastic devotion to smuggling.

Great changes came with the Industrial Revolution, not brought by industry, but by the accompanying social changes and developments in transport. A new and fun-loving lower middle class has arisen, typified by the fictional Mr Pickwick, and Surtees' 'Jorrocks'. Tradesmen and even well-paid artisans had surplus cash and leisure time. All sought occasional relief from the hurly-burly of London life. Royal example made the seaside holiday their aspiration and railways and steam ships brought Thanet within reach.

To serve these visitors a large work-force was recruited, the newcomers being drawn principally from Rural Kent and the London area. Hence, our local accent is a blend of Kentish farm labourer and Cockney sprinkled with Romany-Gypsy and sailor's slang. The resultant building boom blossomed with fine Georgian terraces, whose sadly neglected façades still survive here and there.

As the nineteenth century advanced, the Thanet towns adopted individual characters. Broadstairs, a sleepy fishing village, became a select watering place. Margate, rumbustious favourite of London's *hoi polloi*, grew as a pioneering resort that set the standard for the egalitarian holiday. At Ramsgate a relatively small beach held little for the 'tripper' and the town was dominated by its picturesque but highly mercantile harbour. Professional and middle-class holidaymakers found the town attractive and artists, novelists and celebrities made it their summer home. Birchington, an ancient village, and Westgate, an open field site, both burgeoned into small quiet resorts. The Thanet towns, with a choice of the genteel, the interesting and low-brow fun, all within a few miles, became immensely popular.

Did the locals benefit from this new trade? Arguably not. The holiday trade became a sacred cow with our town councils and many locals saw this as subsidizing the business of a few out of the rates of those the holiday trade tended to impoverish. Until the collapse of the seaside holiday in the 1960s, little effort seemed to be made to bring even light industries to the Island. The old joke was: Thanet life is like a prison sentence, three months' hard labour and nine months' solitary confinement! Just one fringe benefit that the writer can recall with nostalgia, was seeing Hollywood's latest products at the same time as their West End première and at a fraction of the price.

Out in the villages 'the season' was just background noise. Life was no different to that in deepest rural Kent. The farming communities lived almost as much within themselves as in Medieval times and ancient customs such as 'Hoddening' survived. Even in the 1920s a weekly visit to the cinema meant a two hour round trip by pony and trap, and that just from Manston into Ramsgate!

The sea played an important part in Thanet life until well into this century, although it is 400 years since tall ships sailed between the Island and Mainland Kent. Most locals followed the sea at some stage in their lives, or were in some way dependent upon it. The focus of maritime activity was Ramsgate Harbour, an impressive structure even today and important in the days of sail. Built *c.* 1750 as a 'Harbour of Refuge' it did great service. When a gale whipped seas white about the Goodwin Sands, wise captains ran for Ramsgate and dear life. In one storm, it is said, over 400 sail came in for shelter.

Mid-nineteenth-century Ramsgate ranked sixth among Britain's fishing ports and had a thriving timber trade. Ramsgate even had a 'Sailor Town' of dubious repute. This was not as might be expected near the sea front, but around Central and Hill Brow roads and Bolton Street. It was known as the 'Blue Mountains'.

With the Goodwin Sands so near, Ramsgate fishermen were often called upon to mount rescue operations. Luggers or smacks were used until rowing lifeboats were developed, and many lives were saved. It must be said that the men of Margate and Broadstairs were no less valiant, especially since they lacked the Ramsgate boatmen's advantage of being towed out by steam tug. What could happen to the 'Storm Warriors' when they ran out of luck is poignantly illustrated by a monument in St John's cemetery, Margate. It commemorates the crew of the surf-boat, *Friend of all Nations*, lost in an heroic rescue attempt.

Thanet life was particularly eventful in wartime. Most potential invaders saw our coastline as ideal invasion beaches. A 'Great War' contingency plan had the population trekking on foot to Sturry if the 'Huns' came, presumably to hide in the woods. In 1940, a less sanguine or stoical generation took the hint and many left. So reduced was the tempo of life because of this exodus that in some parts of the Island grass grew in the streets. Those who remained 'soldiered on' forming an enthusiastic Home Guard and ARP.

In both World Wars lives and homes were lost through bombing and shelling. During the Second World War Ramsgate's depleted population used an advanced deep shelter system with entrances all over the town. It was just as well since, in one raid alone on 24 August 1940, whole streets were destroyed. On German radio the notorious 'Lord Haw-Haw' (William Joyce) proclaimed that Ramsgate had been obliterated, to the derision of the townsfolk but the great alarm of distant relatives.

Wars are but brief. In the longer sunny years of peace Thanet was no bad place to live, for all its perennial problems of unemployment and low wages. Mild poverty is best endured in beautiful surroundings and the locals at least had those. To the natural splendour of shore and hedgerow (the cabbage prairies were still in the future), were added towns as neat and tasteful as civic pride could make them. A 'local gentry' served the community with imaginative devotion. Their family names are today preserved as those of the parks and gardens they gave us.

Life in old Thanet often had an effervescent quality. There was always something doing, someone new to talk about. Many celebrities made homes here, some drawn from the international avant garde, others renowned for science, daring or wit. There were also politicians. The Island has always had more than its fair share of rebels and eccentrics, and has been home to both inventions and anachronisms. Thus local folk saw such things as gas lighting and the aeroplane long before most of mankind. The world's first fatal motor accident happened at Minster, and Ramsgate boasted Britain's last working sedan chair and practising highwayman.

In these pages the reader will view old Thanet from many perspectives, among them the strange, the quaint and the downright silly. Also detectable is a community loyalty, pride, courage and breadth of view that today's Thanetonians might well strive to emulate.

SECTION ONE

Old Ramsgate

RAMSGATE SANDS at the height of the season. This photograph was taken before the building of the Royal Victoria Pavilion in 1904. In the far background can be seen Ramsgate Harbour station and the Iron Pier.

ELLINGTON PARK with the ornamental fountain. The aviary (the building with the pointed roof) marked the site of the ancient Manor House.

RAMSGATE HIGH STREET showing the façade of 'Lord' George Sanger's Theatre.

THE ROYAL VICTORIA PAVILION, now the 'Tiberius' Casino. The breakwaters are still there but usually covered in sand.

HARBOUR PARADE, note that the road is constructed from wooden blocks as were most streets in down-town Ramsgate.

RAMSGATE FIREMEN with a horse-drawn hand pump, c. 1880.

RAMSGATE FIRE BRIGADE with appliances some time in the early 1930s.

RAMSGATE FIREMEN in front of Ramsgate's Old Town Hall in the late 1920s. This was probably an Armistice Day parade.

THE GRANGE ROAD MILL of Messrs F. and G. English. It had a 16 hp engine as well as wind power.

MASCALL'S WIND AND STREAM MILL, Newington, around 1895.

PEGWELL BAY VILLAGE in the 1900s with the horse-drawn 'brakes' used by sight-seers.

St. Lawrence, Ramsgate.

ST LAWRENCE. This is the High Street looking north-east towards the Wheatsheaf. All the houses to the right were demolished in the 1930s.

PEGWELL BAY in the 1850s. The coastguard sitting on the cliff's edge may be posed but he is wearing authentic uniform. A row of Coastguard Cottages built in the 1840s still stands nearby.

THE BELLEVUE HOTEL at Pegwell (on the cliff-top). The expanse of water in the foreground is an artificial lagoon for sheltered sea-bathing.

THE WORKING MEN'S CONVALESCENT HOME at Pegwell with the sunken garden on reclaimed land behind a sea-wall.

RAMSGATE'S EAST CLIFF looking west, with the Marina Hall (now Nero's) in the foreground and the entrance to the Promenade Pier.

THE PROMENADE PIER in the 1900s. It was well known among anglers and sea trout were often caught there.

THE MARINA BATHING POOL, now filled in, c. 1955.

THE MARINA LIDO and beer garden in the 1950s.

EAST CLIFF PROMENADE with the Granville Hotel and newspaper kiosk.

THE GRANVILLE HOTEL and cliff-top flower beds, c. 1900. Note the well-kept appearance, no graffiti and glass in the shelter windows!

Ramsgate's Royal Harbour

THE CLOCK HOUSE at Ramsgate Harbour in the 1850s. A Royal Navy brig is being worked on in the dry dock which was covered later in the century to form an ice store.

HARBOUR PARADE and shipping in the 1890s.

MILITARY ROAD in the 1860s with fisherman's stores and net lofts.

MILITARY ROAD and the east end of Harbour Parade some time in the 1870s. A paddle-steamer and brigs are on moorings. Just to the left of the Admiral Harvey can be seen Foster's first shipchandler's business. The tall chimney on the extreme left is probably a remnant of Ramsgate's first gasworks run by a local chemist.

THE HARBOUR MASTER'S HOUSE and Trustee's committee rooms in the Pier Yard.

THE HARBOUR MASTER'S HOUSE and attached Customs Store (the 'Droit House'). From the costumes this picture dates from the 1860s.

THE 'SMACK BOYS' HOME' and Jacob's Ladder. The large sailing craft is a collier brig.

MIXED SAILING CRAFT moored against the Military Road. Present are a brig, a Thames barge, a lugger and smacks.

A TOPSAIL SCHOONER moored on the Military Road just below the old Foy Boat Tavern and 'Tidal Ball'. This may be the *Elizabeth Morton*, owned by the Ramsgate Smack Owners Ice Co. and used to bring ice from Norway.

THE SHIPBUILDING YARDS and Pier Gates with a three-masted barque on the main slipway.

A NEAR-DESERTED INNER BASIN in the 1950s. The bowsprit is that of the *Bounty* (once the iron barque *Alor Star*) used as a floating dance hall.

SOME OF RAMSGATE'S SAILING SMACK FLEET.

STEAM TRAWLERS AND DRIFTERS.

THE FISH MARKET. Just visible on the right is part of the ice store built in and over the dry dock.

SMACKSMEN WITH A YOUNG SHARK, probably a Porbeagle (*Lamna cornubica*), a close relative of the 'Great White'.

PLEASURE YACHTS taking on passengers from the Dover Steps on the East Pier, c. 1890.

CAPTAIN WATSON'S PLEASURE YACHT *Moss Rose* outward bound on a trip round the bay, c. 1885.

THE "NEW BRITANNIC" MOTOR LAUNCH, RAMSGATE
UNDER CAPTAIN W. SOLLEY.

JUST A LITTLE SOUVENIR OF THE "NEW BRITANNIC" GAY:
WE'RE VERY GLAD WE'VE MET YOU AND TRUST THE SAME YOU'LL SAY.
WHEN HOLIDAYS ARE OVER AND THE TEARS BEGIN TO DRIP,
MAY YOU AND WE RECALL AGAIN THIS HAPPY LITTLE TRIP!

THE *NEW BRITANNIC* sometimes mixed sight-seeing with a little trawling and the trippers shared the catch.

CAPTAIN SOLLEY AND CREW relaxing between trips. This photograph was taken in the 1950s; note the nearly empty harbour basin and veteran lifeboat in the background.

NEW SIGHTS, NEW SOUNDS: a SRN6 Hovercraft leaves its pad in the harbour basin *en route* to Calais some time in the 1960s.

SECTION THREE

Old Margate

OLD MARGATE SEA FRONT. These cluttered buildings below Fort Hill are remnants of late Georgian Margate. The wooden bridge connected with the base of the Jetty.

FORT ROAD with passing trams.

STROLLERS ON THE JETTY, c. 1900.

THE HOTEL METROPOLE seen from the Jetty. This edifice is chiefly, if unjustly, remembered as the scene of a notorious murder, the case of Sidney Fox.

COASTGUARD COTTAGES AT NEWGATE GAP, c. 1850. Note the old gentleman in his Bath chair.

LONG-VANISHED PAVILIONS on the promenade east of the Jetty.

NEWGATE GAP in the 1900s.

MARGATE FIRE BRIGADE with a horse-drawn hand pump, 1887.

MARGATE FIRE BRIGADE in the 1920s. Sixth from the left is Chief Officer H. Hammond who was decorated for his bravery during the 'Dump Raid' on Ramsgate Harbour on 17 June 1917.

THE OLD COTTAGE HOSPITAL in Victoria Road around the turn of the century. After the Second World War it became Margate Public Library.

PARKING SPACE! Cecil Square in the 1920s showing the façade of the long-vanished Hippodrome, a theatre and cinema.

HOLY TRINITY CHURCH. Built in 1825, it was destroyed by bombing in 1943.

THE ROYAL SCHOOL FOR THE DEAF, Margate, as it appeared in 1879.

WESTBROOK BAY with the Bandstand and Lawns.

WESTBROOK BANDSTAND in the 1890s.

SECTION FOUR

Holidaymakers

RAMSGATE SANDS in the late 1930s. The banner displayed on the boat advertises a coming cinema attraction.

Clock Tower and Sands, Margate.

MARGATE SANDS in the 1920s. It must have felt like something between a football crowd and seal colony.

BATHING AT PALM BAY, CLIFTONVILLE. Note the ornate bathing pavilion.

PADDLING AT MARGATE in 1900. Note the Thames barges against the Pier in the far background.

TIDE'S IN! A strip of Ramsgate Sands below the Royal Victoria Pavilion. Notice the complicated deck-chairs with arm-rests and awnings.

MARGATE SANDS. Note the horse-drawn mobile landing stages used to assist people to embark on bathing machines.

BATHING-MACHINES on Ramsgate Sands. They look vaguely sinister, like a squadron of ancient tanks.

THE BEACH AND PROMENADE AT WESTBROOK with an empty cliff-top vista in the background.

A CONCERT PARTY ENTERTAINS ON THE BEACH AT WESTBROOK. Note that one of the party, on the extreme right, is playing a large harp.

RAMSGATE'S ROYAL VICTORIA PAVILION and Harbour Parade as seen from the East Cliff, c. 1900. A line of cabs and open carriages await fares.

RAMSGATE'S EAST CLIFF, c. 1914. On the beach below is the Marina Bathing Station.

DREAMLAND AMUSEMENT PARK in the 1920s.

AN END OF SEASON FIRE AT DREAMLAND. The locals, ever charitable, said that you could judge the season by the size of the fire!

DONKEY MEN AT NEWGATE GAP.

Boating, Epple Bay, Birchington-on-Sea.

BOAT TRIPS FROM THE BEACH AT EPPLE BAY, c. 1890. It is of interest that these small boats preserve lugger rig.

oat chaises at Cliftonville

GOAT CHAISES AT CLIFTONVILLE. Popular with everybody except the goats.

THE CLIFTONVILLE HYDRO, typical of a number of splendid cliff-top hotels.

DOUBLE BEDROOM WITH PRIVATE BATHROOM, THE HYDRO HOTEL, CLIFTONVILLE
80 BEDROOMS

COX
PHOT

HOTEL SUITE at the Cliftonville Hydro.

DOZING IN THE SUN. Hodge's Flagstaff and Battery, Cliftonville.

THE GUNS OF HODGE'S BATTERY. This 'signalling battery' was quite spurious and the work of a local eccentric. Most of the cannon still exist and range in date from the Napoleonic to Crimean War periods.

MARGATE BATHING BELLES (1930s) in what were thought to be very revealing costumes in their day!

Westgate and Birchington

THE END OF AN ERA. Army and Royal Naval Air Service Officers at the entrance to the St Mildred's Hotel, Westgate, August 1914. They were engaged in setting up a seaplane base before the First World War started.

LADY GUESTS beside the glazed porch of St Mildred's Hotel, Westgate, in 1914. Its proprietor, Sir William Ingram, owned more or less the whole town!

STATION ROAD, Westgate on Sea in the 1900s.

WESTGATE FIRE BRIGADE and a dog mascot with their horse-drawn hand pump in Ethelbert Square, 1885.

WHERE ARE THE HOUSES? The Westgate seaplane base and airfield in 1918, with Garlinge consisting of a few buildings on the horizon. Unknowingly the large slipway was built through the remains of a prehistoric village.

WESTGATE AIRFIELD and Royal Naval Air Service station from the air, 1917.

BIPLANES OF SEVERAL TYPES AT WESTGATE AIRFIELD, 1915. The houses in the far background are in the Westcliff and Rancorn Road area.

A TENTED CAMP at the RNAS station at St Mildred's Bay, Westgate, during the First World War.

AFTER THE WAR. A beach scene at St Mildred's Bay, c. 1920. Only the huge aircraft hanger remains.

ST JAMES' CHURCH, GARLINGE, many years ago. Cows are seen grazing on what is now St James' Park Estate.

THRESHING WITH A STEAM TRACTION ENGINE on a farm at Garlinge in the 1900s.

THE SQUARE, GARLINGE, early this century.

GARLINGE; Rodney Lane looking towards the Square, 1913.

THE SQUARE, BIRCHINGTON, 1937. Idyllic as this scene appears, there were often motor accidents, particularly with the bank holiday traffic.

OFFICIAL OPENING OF THE NEW DRINKING FOUNTAIN, Birchington Square. It is difficult perhaps to imagine how important such fountains and horse-troughs were.

STATION ROAD, BIRCHINGTON, in the 1920s. No parking problems!

MINNIS BAY, BIRCHINGTON, in the 1900s, looking east along the Parade, not long before an old earth-built sea-wall.

MINNIS BAY BEACH SCENE around 1910. The building on the cliff top was the Minnis Bay Hotel.

THE OLD POND, BIRCHINGTON, in the 1920s. This was on the east side of Park Lane.

The Old Cottages and Valley Brooks End, Birchington - on - Sea.

THE BROOK, BROOKS END, BIRCHINGTON, c. 1910. This still exists, although today only a dike. It drained a valley leading east to Acol which is crowded with remains of ancient settlements.

The Villages

HUNTSMEN AND PACK AT THE CROWN INN, SARRE, c. 1910. This ancient inn is a last vestige of the old port of Sarre with its church and manor house that John Lewis described as a 'town' in 1723.

THE SARRE POSTMISTRESS. Mrs Smith taking the air outside her shop and sub-post office in late Victorian days.

Below:
SARRE WINDMILL at the turn of the century. Just inches below the feet of the man in the foreground are the graves of a pagan Anglo-Saxon cemetery.

The Old Mill at Sarre

THE CHURCH AT ST NICHOLAS-AT-WADE, from an early nineteenth-century engraving.

THE STREET looking north-west towards the church, c. 1900.

A FARM WORKER RELAXING. Mr W. Law with his accordion outside his home at Shuart Farm Cottages, St Nicholas, in the 1930s.

AN ANCIENT TRADITION REVIVED, modern Hoodeners outside the Bell Inn, at St Nicholas, in 1966. The Hooden or Hodden Horse ceremony ceased in 1914 but was resumed within the span of living memory.

THE OLD VICARAGE at St Nicholas in the 1920s.

IVY COTTAGE on the marshes at Wagtail Farm, St Nicholas, in the 1900s.

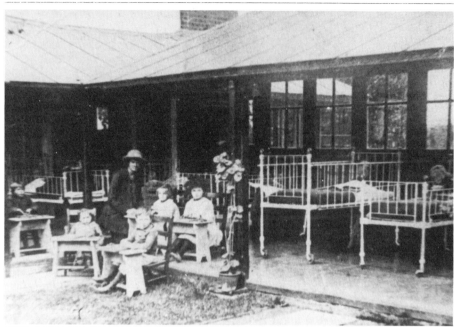

OPEN-AIR ISOLATION WARD at the Hospital, St Nicholas, in the 1920s. The glum children would probably rather be back at school infecting everybody!

THE HOSPITAL, ST NICHOLAS, from the south side.

FARM WORKER MR W. LAW brings a waggon-load of straw up Shuart Lane, St Nicholas, in the 1930s.

PACKHAM'S, the village general store at St Nicholas in the 1920s.

MONKTON, a street scene at the turn of the century.

A HUGE CHALK PIT (long in-filled) at Tothill Street, Minster, 1920s. On the horizon is the grim grisly old 'Minster Spike' – a feared and hated workhouse.

MINSTER VILLAGE HALL in the 1920s.

CHURCH STREET, MINSTER, at the turn of the century. Note the unmetalled road surface which must have been a quagmire in winter.

ACOL HILL, looking south towards the Crown and Sceptre Inn, probably photographed around 1910. Note the rustic fence and corn stooks.

HARVESTING LAVENDER at Monkton in the 1900s. The shrub was much used as a toiletry and clothes-moth repellent.

Traders and Commerce

BEGINNING OF A LITTLE EMPIRE. Foster's ship chandlers store in York Street, Ramsgate, in the 1880s. This is not the shop that some now living will remember (the site of Tesco's doorway) but on the east side at the back of the Admiral Harvey.

BRINGING COALS. Perry's (coal merchants) schooner *Old Goody* unloading at Ramsgate, 1890. Their business was at No. 66 High Street.

MAKING SMOKE. Georgiana Crow's tobacco shop in Ramsgate, 1885.

GROCERY EMPORIUM. Pilcher Page & Co., King Street, Ramsgate, (telephone no. 17). They needed a $2\frac{1}{2}$ hp engine just to grind each day's fresh roasted coffee.

SEATS FOR THE CUSTOMERS! Inside Pilcher and Page's shop.

PRYCE & JUDD, ship chandlers and Ironmongers, No. 24 Queen Street, Ramsgate. The ancient York Tavern situated in York Street can be seen on the extreme left.

FLEET'S BREWERY, Broad Street, Ramsgate, (formerly Austen's). Only the finest Thanet barley used. Best 'light bitter' delivered at 1s. (5p), per gallon, (1895 prices).

SMALL SHOP. The modest display of Philpott, family butcher, in High Street, St Lawrence, 1890.

BIG BUSINESS! Display by A.T. Richford, butcher, whose shop stood on the corner of Meeting Street with High Street, Ramsgate. Next door was the Temperance Hotel.

TEA AT 1s. 6d. (7½p) A POUND! An advertisement by F.W. Pointer, wholesale grocer, No. 63 King Street, Ramsgate, 1890s.

J.H. HOPE, pastry-cook and confectioner, No. 26 Addington Street, Ramsgate, 1893. 'A display of toothsome delicacies tempting the appetite of the observer.'

SECTION EIGHT

Inns and Public Houses

THE HONEYSUCKLE INN in the 1900s. This pub is situated just off Hereson Road, Ramsgate. It has changed very little externally since the photograph was taken. Up the hill and behind the pub one or two of the ancient cottages that once formed the hamlet of Hereson still remain. One of them has traces of fifteenth-century stonework.

THE BROWN JUG at Dumpton. While within the boundaries of Broadstairs it was obviously thought of as 'near Ramsgate' when this and the photograph below were taken.

THE 'FAMOUS' THREE-LEGGED PIG being shown off by her owner, the proprietor of the Brown Jug.

THE BELL INN, High Street, Minster. A tea-garden is advertised.

THE HUSSAR HOTEL, GARLINGE. An enthusiasm for advertising is noticeable, including bird seed and parrot food. Did they sell it inside?

THE KING'S HEAD at Sarre, around 1910, and claiming to be the 'Half Way House'. Notice that they had a garage facility.

THE CROWN INN AT SARRE. At pains to point out to its nearby rival the King's Head that it is '*The Old Established* Half Way House'. Like its rival it is involving itself with the motor car.

THE BELL INN at St Nicholas at Wade, c. 1880.

THE CHILTON TAVERN at Pegwell Road, Ramsgate, in 1914.

WHO WERE THESE MEN? In the background, a stable in the Chilton Tavern yard sports a Goodyear Tyre advertisement.

Events and Occasions

THE STONE-LAYING CEREMONY for a 'New Orphanage' in Harold Road, Cliftonville, in 1874.

LAYING THE FOUNDATION STONE for Margate General Hospital in 1929.

THE HUSTINGS! Ramsgate people took elections very seriously in the early 1900s.

A SEA-ANGLING COMPETITION between mayors of the Thanet towns in the 1950s. In spite of the smiles, these could be real Toytown v Arkville needle matches.

A CHANCE MEETING between Sir Umah Hayat (leader of the Twahanas of the Punjab) and Henry Smith of Nether Hale Farm, at a local farming show in the 1930s. Are they talking about horses?

Feb-2ⁿᵈ 1914.

PATIENTS AT THE WORKING MEN'S CONVALESCENT HOME, Pegwell, about to embark on an outing. Note the solid tyres of the charabanc.

WIRELESS TELEGRAPHY PERSONNEL (radio operators) at the RNAS Air Station, Westgate-on-Sea, 1918.

THE OFFICIAL OPENING OF A RECREATION HUT at Manston Airfield, July 1916. Young town-bred personnel complained of the eerie quiet and dark nights at this lonely spot!

READING A PROCLAMATION in Cecil Square, Margate, around 1900. Notice the 'boater' hats worn by the men of the Royal Navy detachment.

THE MAYOR OF MARGATE addresses a group in Cecil Square. Are these men volunteers going to the Boar War or returning heroes? Note the East Kent Yeomanry uniforms.

HUNTSMEN AT SARRE in the 1900s.

SOCIAL INTERLUDE during a coursing meeting at Nether Hale Farm, Birchington, in the early 1920s.

PREPARATION FOR A BURIAL AT SEA at the Dover Steps, Ramsgate Harbour, some time early this century. A not uncommon ceremony when Britain was still the premier maritime nation.

HARD HAT DIVERS at work on the lock-gates of Ramsgate Harbour basin, 1920s.

A HARBOUR TRAGEDY. This steam trawler sank at her moorings near the old fish market at Ramsgate Harbour. A crew member who was sleeping aboard was drowned. It happened in the 1920s, just before the trawler fleet left Ramsgate for Brixham and the western ports.

'AS REAPS THE WILD WIND'. When great storms crash upon Thanet's shores they usually blow from north or east, the exceptions being the tempests of 1703 and 1987. A great storm in 1897 brought this havoc to Margate's old sea front. Note the sea-wall below Fort Point.

STORM DAMAGE in 1897. Notice that these long vanished sea front buildings stood on piles.

THE SAME SCENE looking inland. Part of Cobbs Brewery and the Britannia Inn can be seen on the cliff top. The building with a chimney is probably a laundry.

THE MORNING AFTER. This is all that remained of Margate Jetty after a great storm in 1978. More than a decade later the 'extension', where once paddle-steamers docked, survives as mute witness to Victorian engineering skill.

People

GOTCHER! Is this occupant of the ancient stocks at Monkton a real 'gentleman of the road' posing for a handout or just one of the villagers fooling about?

SQUADRON COMMANDER CHARLES HENRY BUTLER DSO DSC at Manston in 1917. He led the Royal Naval Air Service War Flight that operated against German air raiders during the Zeppelin and Gotha offensives.

THE PUBLICAN AND STAFF OF THE CHILTON TAVERN, Ramsgate, 1914. The stuffed birds were commonplace decorations, the Shakespeare at Ramsgate had so many 'it was like drinking in Quex Park Museum'!

ST NICHOLAS HOODENERS in 1913. The ancient ceremony of parading the Hooden (or Hodden) Horse with songs and music was rooted in pagan Saxon England, probably as the 'Odin Horse'.

HOODENERS at St Nicholas early this century. The 'vulgar practise' died out at St Lawrence in Victorian times and lay dormant at St Nicholas for a time but has since been revived.

THE FOUNDING FATHER at the centre of the picture is W.T. Foster who set up as a ship chandler in York Street, Ramsgate, in the 1870s. The glum young man at bottom right is Herbert Foster who sold penny fish-hooks to countless Ramsgate boys – the author among them.

April 16th 1914

'IF THE DEVIL COULD CAST HIS NET'. Patrons of the Chilton Tavern about to embark on a charabanc outing. Any bets on the first port of call?

THE MARGATE TOWN CRIER. This badly damaged print shows the last holder of the office at work in the Market Place.

THE MEN OF WESTGATE FIRE BRIGADE with presentation cups, some time in the 1890s.

THREE OLD RAMSGATE SMACKSMEN photographed in the Pier Yard at the turn of the century.

FLIGHT LIEUTENANT GEOFFREY BROMET, (later Sir Geoffrey Bromet) at the Royal Naval Air Service station at Westgate-on-Sea, 1914.

DR ARTHUR ROWE, 1858–1926, an eminent physician, palaentologist and local historian – one of Thanet's most distinguished sons. He was the first to carry out 'rescue archaeology' in Thanet and his will bestowed a valuable collection, known as the Rowe Bequest, on Margate.

ARCHAEOLOGICAL DISCOVERIES behind the Britannia Hotel, Fort Hill, Margate. Roman building remains and burials were found.

DR ROWE'S HOME at Shottendane Road, Margate, later the Railwaymen's Convalescent Home. The upper floor was the doctor's museum of local archaeology.

MEN OF MARGATE FIRE BRIGADE with a cup, 1920s.

MARGATE FIREMEN with appliances at the old fire station off King Street, 1950s.

SEA SCOUTS at Westgate-on-Sea, 1915.

SEA ROVERS. The arrival of the Viking ship *Hugin* at Ramsgate Harbour in 1949. It was built by a group of Danes who rowed it across the North Sea and today it stands on the cliff-top at Pegwell Bay.

THE CREW OF THE RAMSGATE LIFEBOAT *PRUDENTIAL* who took their boat to the Dunkirk beaches in 1940.

RAMSGATE LIFEBOAT CREW and families on a charabanc outing at Minster in the 1920s.

Methods of Transport

THE LAST OF COMMERCIAL SAIL. A Thames barge rounding the head of the West Pier at Ramsgate Harbour. For 150 years, ending in the 1950s, these vessels brought bulk cargoes to Thanet.

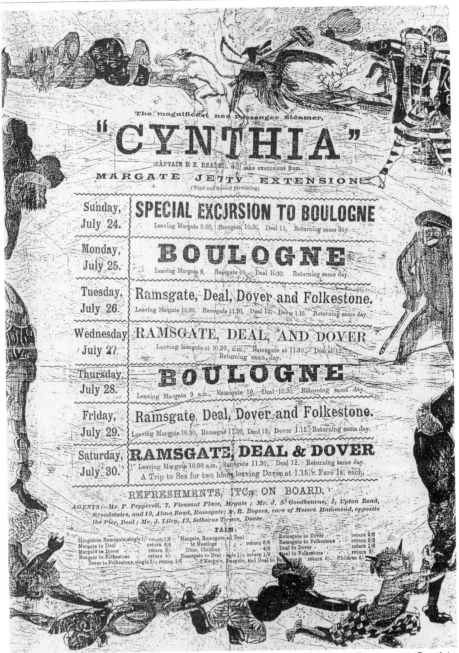

The magnificent new Passenger Steamer,

"CYNTHIA"

(CAPTAIN E. E. READE), will make excursions from

MARGATE JETTY EXTENSION

(Wind and weather permitting).

Sunday, July 24.	**SPECIAL EXCURSION TO BOULOGNE** Leaving Margate 9.30, Ramsgate 10.30, Deal 11, Returning same day.
Monday, July 25.	**BOULOGNE** Leaving Margate 9, Ramsgate 10, Deal 10.30. Returning same day.
Tuesday, July 26.	**Ramsgate, Deal, Dover and Folkestone.** Leaving Margate 10.30, Ramsgate 11.30, Deal 12, Dover 1.15. Returning same day.
Wednesday July 27.	**RAMSGATE, DEAL, AND DOVER** Leaving Margate at 10.30, a.m., Ramsgate at 11.30, Deal at 12. Returning same day.
Thursday, July 28.	**BOULOGNE** Leaving Margate 9 a.m., Ramsgate 10, Deal 10.30. Returning same day.
Friday, July 29.	**Ramsgate, Deal, Dover and Folkestone.** Leaving Margate 10.30, Ramsgate 11.30, Deal 12, Dover 1.15. Returning same day.
Saturday, July 30.	**RAMSGATE, DEAL & DOVER** Leaving Margate 10.30 a.m., Ramsgate 11.30, Deal 12. Returning same day. A Trip to Sea for two hours leaving Dover at 1.15. Fare 1s. each.

REFRESHMENTS, &c., ON BOARD.

AGENTS:—Mr. P. Pepperell, 7, Pleasant Place, Margate ; Mr. J. S. Goodbourne, 1, Upton Road, Broadstairs, and 13, Alma Road, Ramsgate; Mr. R. Rogers, care of Messrs. Hammond, opposite the Pier, Deal ; Mr. J. Liley, 12, Selborne Terrace, Dover.

FARES :—

Margate to Ramsgate, single 1/- return 1/6	Margate, Ramsgate, and Deal	Ramsgate to Dover ... return 2/6
Margate to Deal ... return 2/6	... to Hastings ... return 6/6	Ramsgate to Folkestone ... return 3/6
Margate to Dover ... return 3/-	Ditto, Children ... 4/6	Deal to Dover ... return 1/6
Margate to Folkestone ... return 4/-	Ramsgate to Deal - single 1/- return 1/6	Deal to Folkestone ... return 2/-
Dover to Folkestone, single 1/- return 1/6	Margate, Ramsgate, And Deal to Boulogne return 6/- Children 4/-	

A STEAMER POSTER. Even before the railways, vessels such as the paddle-steamer *Cynthia* opened up Thanet to holidaymakers. This poster dates from 1882.

THE OPENING OF MARGATE JETTY EXTENSION in 1877. This made landing from the paddle-steamers a safer and more comfortable business.

MARGATE JETTY and Steamer Landing in 1897. A regatta is in progress, note that only working boats are present, not quite a yachting occasion?

THE PADDLE-STEAMER *ROYAL SOVEREIGN* coming into Ramsgate Harbour, c. 1900.

GROVE FERRY with a tiny steam launch alongside the ferry pontoon. While this is not in Thanet, it illustrates a hazard of one route into Thanet in the early days of motoring.

THE *GRANVILLE EXPRESS* coming through Garlinge Crossing at speed, c. 1910. The crossing was closed in 1923.

RAMSGATE'S FIRST STATION built by the South Eastern Railway Co. in 1846. The old station wall can still be seen at the junction of Margate Road and Station Approach.

RAMSGATE SANDS STATION built by the London Chatham and Dover Railway Company in 1859. It still stands as the 'Pleasurama' building.

RAMSGATE SANDS STATION from the East Cliff, with an army of bathing-machines in the background.

A TRAIN ABOUT TO ENTER THE TUNNEL. This impressive piece of engineering linked Ramsgate Sands station with Broadstairs via a cutting at Dumpton.

A LONDON CHATHAM AND DOVER M3 Class engine at Ramsgate Sands station.

WAR SERVICE. One of the engines that operated on the spur-line connecting Birchington with Manston Airfield at the close of the First World War.

RAMSGATE TO MINSTER FOR 5p! One of the horse buses or 'brakes' that operated the first 'mystery trips'. Some were horse-drawn pub crawls.

NOT TODAY THANK YOU! This elegant vehicle belonged to a Birchington undertaker.

A HORSE BUS in Station Road, Westgate, at the turn of the century.

A TRAM DESCENDING MADEIRA WALK, RAMSGATE. Occasionally the brakes failed on such hills with dire results.

HORSE BUSES AND TRAMS at Margate Harbour.

TRAMS AND A CROWDED BANDSTAND at Wellington Crescent, Ramsgate, around 1910.

A RARE BIRD for those days. This seaplane, a Short 126, put down at Ramsgate on 30 July 1914.

A SHORT T5 BIPLANE at Cliftonville in 1912. What did some of the elderly spectators think of it?

A PUBLICITY STUNT. A Fairey Seaplane leaving Westgate-on-Sea with a special mail delivery in 1920.

A NEW SIGHT FOR RAMSGATE (and the rest of the world for that matter). A Westland SRN6 Hovercraft returns from a scheduled trip to Calais in 1966.

Schools both High and Humble

A POIGNANT GROUP. Boys of the 1st XI, Godwin College, Cliftonville, 1914. How many were alive in 1919?

ST NICHOLAS LODGE, a private boarding school, c. 1908. The school boasted its own generating equipment, a comment on the reliability of the electricity supply at that time.

St. Nicholas Lodge, nr. Birchington-on-Sea. The Washing Room

THE WASHING ROOM at St Nicholas Lodge. The facility looks somewhat spartan by today's standards.

AN INFANTS' CLASS in the Primary School, St Nicholas at Wade, c. 1910.

VILLAGE SCHOOL PUPILS at St Nicholas in the 1900s.

'TOWNLEY CASTLE' a private school at Chatham Street, Ramsgate, c. 1880. It was formerly home to an Indian Prince who kept an elephant in the garden!

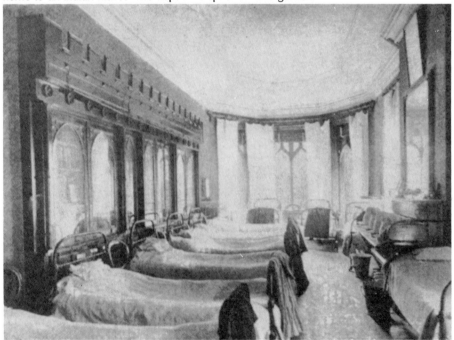

A PALATIAL DORMITORY at Townley Castle School.

THE SOUTH EASTERN COLLEGE, Ramsgate, now St Lawrence College. Founded in 1879, it had many innovative assets, such as a large indoor swimming pool and its own fire brigade.

THE DINING HALL and Junior School, South Eastern College, c. 1895.

CHATHAM HOUSE, FRONT VIEW.

CHATHAM HOUSE COLLEGE, Ramsgate (now Chatham House Grammar School). The imposing gateway of Townley Castle College is shown on the left of this wood engraving.

THE FIRST ELEVEN (and dog) Chatham House College, 1894.

War Damage and Defences

THE GUN BATTERY ON RAMSGATE'S EAST CLIFF midway through the Second World War. They are six-inch naval guns in steel turrets backed by reinforced concrete blast shelters.

LUCKY SURVIVORS. The woman on the right slept elsewhere on the night of 18 March 1917 when her bedroom was hit by one of the first shells fired on Ramsgate.

CHILD CASUALTIES. The funeral at St Luke's Church, Ramsgate, of children killed nearby in a bombing raid, March 1916.

UNEXPLODED BOMBS dropped in a night-raid on Ramsgate, May 1915. The author's mother remembers being allowed to hold one of these projectiles.

REVENGE, the remains of a 'Gotha' bomber shot down at Hartsdown, Margate. Relics of the plane are kept at Quex Park Museum.

BOMB DAMAGE IN ALBERT STREET, Ramsgate. A result of the 'Dump Raid' in June 1917. An ammunition dump at the Harbour was hit by Zeppelin bombs.

RAMSGATE GASWORKS after bombing on 31 October 1917.

A MOTOR GUNBOAT moored against the West Pier at Ramsgate Harbour in the First World War.

AA GUN CREW aboard the gunboat practice in readiness for air raids.

IN THE BEGINNING. Manston Aerodrome as a Royal Naval Air Service Station in the First World War. Twenty-five years on it would have the longest runway in the world and be able to accept hundreds of returning bombers in a day.

A FLYING-BOAT AT WESTGATE RNAS BASE in 1919. This aircraft (a 'Coastal Experimental 1') was an advanced and streamlined design that compares well with some built 20 years later.

BOMB DAMAGE at Albion Place, Ramsgate, 17 May 1917.

RAMSGATE ARP HEAVY RESCUE SQUAD with tender in Cannon Road car park in 1943. The writer's father is standing on the extreme left.

A BOFORS GUN EMPLACEMENT on the East Cliff at Ramsgate in 1944.

THE CREW OF 'THOR' a 3.7 inch anti-aircraft gun, West Cliff, Ramsgate, 1942.

DEFENCES AT WELLINGTON CRESCENT on the East Cliff, Ramsgate, 1944.

BARBED-WIRE WEEDS AND CAMOUFLAGE at Wellington Crescent. The 'wooden shed' in front of the bandstand is, in fact, a concrete pillbox fitted with a mock roof.

CLOSED FOR THE DURATION. The newspaper kiosk near the Granville Hotel.

OPENING SOON! Workmen demolishing defences at the entrance to the Marina Bathing Pool.

ANTI-INVASION DEFENCES on Ramsgate Sands.

CLEARING THE DEFENCES in 1945 required great care. Ramsgate Sands yielded tons of explosives, both British and German.

IT WAS EASIER TO PUT UP! Demolishing a concrete pillbox in St Augustine's Road, Ramsgate.

A PILLBOX ON THE EAST PIER at Ramsgate Harbour. Note the massive construction.

QUICK, THE SEASON STARTS IN THREE WEEKS! The Esplanade, Ramsgate, 1945.

Thanet Men at Arms

MEN OF THE EAST KENT YEOMANRY at training camp in 1912. Most of them would have been recruited from Thanet's farming community.

BEWARE DAD'S ARMY! Men of Ramsgate LDV (Home Guard), looking impressively efficient as they pose with their Vickers machine guns somewhere in Ramsgate, c. 1943.

FULL STRENGTH. A combined parade of Thanet's Home Guard, ARP, Firemen and Special
Constables in the grounds of Chatham House School, Ramsgate, probably in 1943.

SOME RAMSGATE HOME GUARDS at Cannon Road car park, Ramsgate. A Depot?

RAMSGATE HOME GUARDS parade in battle order, West Cliff, Ramsgate, 1945.

STANDING DOWN. A last line up by Ramsgate's Home Guard in front of the West Cliff Bandstand (now a boating pool).

The Lifeboat Tradition

A LAUNCHING CEREMONY for a Ramsgate lifeboat, the *Charles and Susanna Stephens*. Between 1905 and 1926 the boat and its crew saved 294 lives.

HAMMING IT UP. Ramsgate 'Storm Warriors' going a little over the top for the photographer. The man with the telescope is actually looking inland!

ALFRED PAGE the skipper of the steam tugs *Vulcan* and *Aid* that were used to tow the 'Bradford' series of lifeboats to such rescues as that of the *Indean Chief*.

HEROES IN OLD AGE. Survivors of the famous *Indean Chief* rescue of 1881 pictured in 1926. Left to right: David Berry (82), Thomas Friend (82), Henry Belsey (83), Charles Verrion (80) and Thomas Cooper (80).

AN OLD MARGATE LIFEBOAT, perhaps the *Quiver*.

THE MARGATE LIFEBOAT *North Foreland* on the slip of the Jetty boat-house.

GOODBYE TO SAIL AND OARS. Ramsgate's *Prudential* under power. Between 1926 and 1953 she saved 330 lives.

THE *MICHAEL AND LILY DAVIS* on her moorings. She served from 1953 to 1976 and saved 309 lives.

ACKNOWLEDGEMENTS

Some of the photographs used in this book were collected by the writer over many years. Others were the gift of two old friends and local historians, the late Messrs Charles Busson and David Scurrell. Most of those relating to Ramsgate Harbour belong to East Kent Maritime Museum. I should like to also thank the following individuals:

The late Mr William J. Cole • Mr Tristan Jones • Mr William Lapthorne
Mr John Ray • Mrs Jill Smith • Mr George Slade • Mr David Steed
Mr Robert Varnham • Mr Geoffrey Williams.